What W[illegible] Weather Be?

by Kathy Furgang

MW01689202

What is the weather like today? Is it rainy or sunny? Is it hot or cold?

The weather changes every day. It also changes from season to season.

People use a lot of information to predict what the weather will be like. When you predict, you make a good guess about something.

▲ This man is collecting information about the weather.

▲ These people are using information to predict the weather.

People use information from the past to predict the weather.

This chart shows what the weather was like in the winter in Maine. People can use this information to predict what the weather will be in Maine this winter.

Can you predict what the winter will be in Maine this year? Can you predict what the winter will be like five years from now?

Maine in Winter

2003	cold and snowy
2002	cold and snowy
2001	cold and snowy
2000	cold and snowy
1999	cold and snowy

This chart shows temperatures in a California city. It shows how hot it was on most days in July over the past five years.

Can you predict what the temperature will be on most days next July? Will it be closer to 65 or 75 degrees?

July
in San Francisco, California

Year	Temperature (°F)
2003	67 degrees
2002	65 degrees
2001	67 degrees
2000	62 degrees
1999	65 degrees

This chart shows how much rain three cities get every year.

▲ Chicago

Predict which city will get about 35 inches of rain next year.

◀ Phoenix

Rainfall

City and State	Inches of Rain
New Orleans, Louisiana	6 inches
Phoenix, Arizona	8 inches
Chicago, Illinois	36 inches

◀ New Orleans

This map shows about how much snow each city gets every winter.

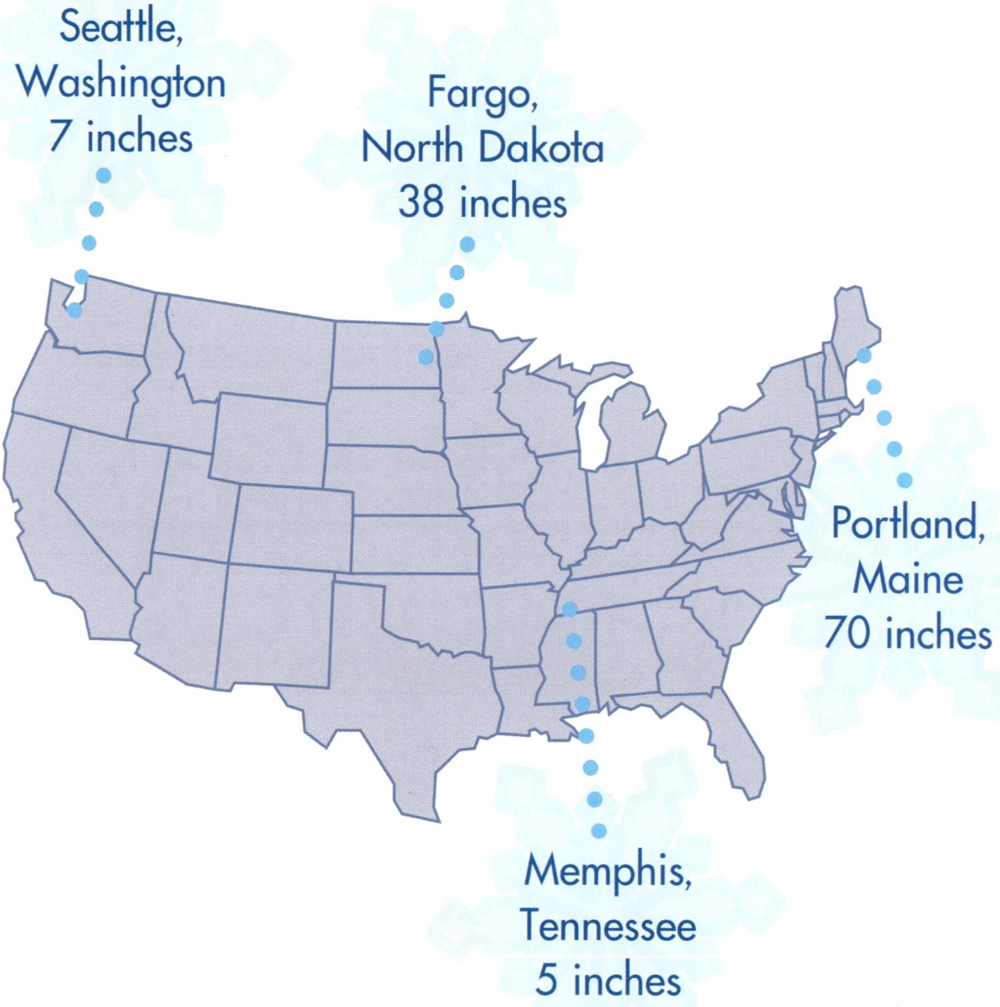

Predict which city will have the most snow next year. Why do you think so?

Knowing the weather helps people in many ways. It helps people get ready for storms.

It helps people
like farmers and pilots
do their jobs.

It also helps people know how to dress. And it helps them know what they can do outdoors!